ALTERNATOR
BOOKS™

CRYPTOLOGY

SECRETS OF
STEGANOGRAPHY

RACHAEL L. THOMAS

Lerner Publications ◆ Minneapolis

Lerner Publications Company
An imprint of Lerner Publishing Group, Inc.
241 First Avenue North
Minneapolis, MN 55401 USA

For reading levels and more information, look up this title at www.lernerbooks.com.

Main body text set in Aptifer Sans LT Pro
Typeface provided by Linotype

The images in this book are used with the permission of: © Mirrorpix/Getty Images, pp. 3, 18; © giannimarchetti/Getty Images, p. 4; © Leemage/Getty Images, p. 5; © Federal Bureau of Investigation, pp. 6, 19, 26; © studioportosabbia/Getty Images, p. 7; © South_agency/Getty Images, p. 8; © Alexander Supertramp/Shutterstock Images, p. 9; © sedmak/Getty Images, p. 10; © Dhoxax/Getty Images, p. 11; © ZU_09/Getty Images, p. 12; © Mondadori Portfolio/Getty Images, p. 13; © adoc-photos/Getty Images, p. 14; © shellhawker/Getty Images, p. 15; © UniversalImagesGroup/Getty Images, pp. 16–17; © Popperfoto/ Getty Images, pp. 20–21; © REDPIXEL.PL/Shutterstock Images, p. 22; © w-ings/Getty Images, p. 23; © Everett Collection/Shutterstock Images, p. 24; © santypan/Getty Images, p. 25; © ALEXANDER NEMENOV/Getty Images, p. 27; © Iurii Motov/Shutterstock Images, p. 28; © Mighty Media, Inc., p. 29 (all).

Cover Photo: © Gwengoat/Getty Images

Design Elements: © AF-studio/Getty Images; © 4khz/Getty Images; © non-exclusive/Getty Images

Library of Congress Cataloging-in-Publication Data

Names: Thomas, Rachael L., author.
Title: Secrets of steganography / Rachael L. Thomas.
Description: Minneapolis, Minnesota : Lerner Publications, [2022] | Series: Cryptology (Alternator books) | Audience: Ages 8–12. | Audience: Grades 4–6. | Summary: "Steganography is the art of concealing messages in plain sight. Read about invisible inks, the Cardan Grille, the use of microdots in WWI, and the butterfly maps of Lord Baden-Powell"— Provided by publisher.
Identifiers: LCCN 2020019914 (print) | LCCN 2020019915 (ebook) | ISBN 9781728404622 (library binding) | ISBN 9781728417998 (ebook)
Subjects: LCSH: Cryptography—History—Juvenile literature. | Ciphers—History—Juvenile literature.
Classification: LCC Z103.3 .T474 2021 (print) | LCC Z103.3 (ebook) | DDC 652/.8—dc23

LC record available at https://lccn.loc.gov/2020019914
LC ebook record available at https://lccn.loc.gov/2020019915

Manufactured in the United States of America
1-48520-49034-12/7/2020

TABLE OF
CONTENTS

INTRODUCTION

It is 499 BCE in the ancient Greek city of Miletus. The city's leader, Aristagoras, is unhappy. Aristagoras's father-in-law, Histiaeus, used to lead the city. But he has been imprisoned by the Persian Empire. The empire controls Miletus. So, Aristagoras must lead the city in Histiaeus's place.

Suddenly, Aristagoras learns that a secret message has arrived from Histiaeus. A slave is brought to Aristagoras. To see the message, the slave tells him, Aristagoras will have to shave the slave's head.

City officials shave the slave's hair. As they do, letters are revealed. Histiaeus has tattooed a message across the slave's scalp. Soon, the full message is revealed: "Revolt." Aristagoras nods. It is time to take his city back from Persian rule.

King Darius I (*top*) ruled Persia in 499 BCE.

In ancient Greece and Rome, slaves were often tattooed as punishment.

WHAT IS STEGANOGRAPHY?

Steganography is the art of hiding messages in plain sight. People must know where and how to look if they want to find information hidden using steganography.

Steganography is closely related to cryptology. Cryptology is the science of secret communication. It involves creating codes and ciphers that conceal the meaning of secret messages. Messages that have been concealed using a code or cipher are called cryptograms.

Someone who tries to crack a cryptogram knows that it holds secret information. The aim of steganography, however, is to keep someone from knowing that there is a secret to learn.

In the 1940s, a spy used this doll to smuggle tiny, secret photographs into Germany.

This image might look normal. However, it could contain information hidden using steganography.

The Federal Bureau of Investigation (FBI) solves digital crimes associated with steganography and cryptology.

Steganography is the process of concealing a message. The process of searching for and revealing hidden information is called steganalysis.

These words fell out of use in the early 1800s. The word "steganography" was even removed from dictionaries! Dictionary makers decided that steganography was simply an old-fashioned word for cryptology.

Messages can be hidden in audio files, image files, and more using steganography.

However, modern experts recognize that steganography is different from cryptology. This distinction became more obvious with the development of digital technologies, such as computers.

Modern steganographers can hide secret information in digital files that otherwise seem normal. These techniques have opened the door to a new kind of secret communication, and a new kind of digital crime.

ANCIENT STEGANOGRAPHY

The first use of steganography was documented by the ancient Greek historian Herodotus. Herodotus wrote many stories about the Persian Wars of the fifth century BCE. During this time, the Persian and Greek empires fought for dominance.

Around 500 BCE, city leader Histiaeus was being held captive by the Persian king. Meanwhile, his son-in-law, Aristagoras, led the Greek city of Miletus.

Histiaeus wished to send a secret message to Aristagoras encouraging him to rebel against Miletus's Persian rulers. So, he shaved the head of a slave and tattooed a message on the slave's scalp! Histiaeus waited for the slave's hair to grow back. Then, he sent the slave to Aristagoras.

Herodotus is often called the father of history.

The ruins of Miletus are in modern-day Turkey.

The Persian King Xerxes (*right*) ordered much of Athens to be burned in the 480 BCE attack.

In 480 BCE, the Persian army launched an attack on Athens, Greece. The Persians believed their attack would be a surprise. But a Greek soldier named Demaratus had used wax tablets to sneak a warning to the city.

Wax tablets were often used to conduct business and complete schoolwork in ancient times.

A wax tablet was a wooden board covered in wax. Writers used a sharp tool to scratch letters into the wax. After use, the wax was melted and replaced.

Demaratus hid his message by scratching it into the wood of several tablets. Then, he covered the message with wax. The "blank" writing tablets later arrived in Athens. Officials scratched off the wax and revealed the message beneath! Demaratus's warning helped Athens prepare for the Persian attack.

Philo of Byzantium

Invisible ink is one of the oldest forms of steganography. The Greek scientist Philo of Byzantium created the first invisible ink recipe around the third century BCE.

Philo's recipe used tannic acid from gall nuts. The acid is transparent. But it turns black when mixed with the chemical compound iron sulfate.

Philo suggested writing a secret message with gall nut ink. Then, the recipient would brush the paper with iron sulfate. This would cause a chemical reaction, revealing the message.

STEAM Spotlight—Science

Many heat-activated invisible inks are made with lemon, apple, or onion juice. Heat breaks down compounds in these acidic juices and releases carbon, which then turns brown. A message written with heat-activated ink will not be visible at first. But heating the paper slightly will make the message appear in brown script!

Gall nuts are ball-shaped growths
found on certain oak trees.

STEGANOGRAPHY IN WAR

L ord Robert Baden-Powell was a British spy in the early 1900s. He worked in what is now Croatia. Baden-Powell reported the region's military activity to the British government. Baden-Powell disguised himself and his reports by pretending to be a butterfly collector. He sketched pictures of butterflies with detailed wing patterns. The drawings did not look suspicious. But they used steganography to communicate secret information! Lines on the butterflies' wings were actually maps. Shapes on the wings represented gun postings. Different shapes represented different types of guns.

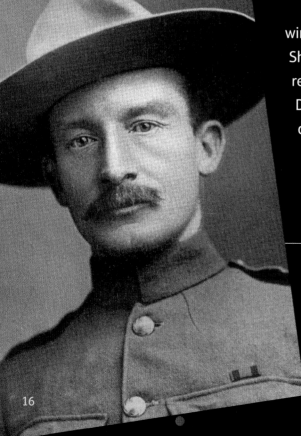

Lord Baden-Powell founded the Boy Scout movement in 1908. This led to the development of the Boy Scouts of America in 1910.

CRYPTO SPOTLIGHT

The Cardan Grille is a well-known steganography technique. It was invented by Italian mathematician Gerolamo Cardano in 1550. A grille is a piece of paper or thin metal with holes in it. The holes look random but are carefully planned. When placed over a specific page of writing, the grille's holes show only certain words, revealing a secret message.

Gerolamo Cardano

A Minox Spy Camera

During World War I (1914–1918), countries used many different methods to communicate secretly. One method was microdots. Microdots are tiny photographs. Some are just 0.05 inches (0.1 cm) in diameter! Microdots were often hidden in writing as punctuation. Recipients could view them using a microscope.

Special cameras were used to create microdots. The most common was the Minox Spy Camera. Spies used it to take pictures of secret documents to create microdots.

CRYPTO SPOTLIGHT

During World War II (1939–1945), Velvalee Dickinson was caught spying for the Japanese in the United States. Dickinson ran a doll store in New York. She sent doll invoices to Japanese agents. These letters secretly provided information about US ships under repair in local shipyards. Dickinson described the ships as if they were dolls. For example, she called an aircraft carrier with an anti-submarine net a fisherman doll carrying a net.

Dickinson's doll store

Three microdots used to communicate with a Russian spy ring in the 1960s

To make a microdot, spies first used a microdot camera to take a thumbnail-sized picture. The picture was photographed a second time through a reverse microscope. This reduced the photograph to a fraction of an inch in size. Spies dropped the microdot over a dotted feature in a letter. Finally, the microdot was glued in place using a photography chemical called collodion.

For a while, microdots hid information effectively. However, microdots were very shiny. Secrets agents eventually learned to look for them by holding letters up to the light.

STEAM Spotlight—Science

Collodion is a chemical compound made by soaking cotton in nitric and sulfuric acids. The cotton is then dissolved in alcohol. A thin layer of collodion creates a clear, flexible coating as it dries. In addition to gluing microdots in place, people have also used this compound for closing wounds.

An enlarged microdot showing Russian writing

...БУДЕТ В КОНЦЕ МЕСЯЦА...АДАЛ ОТ ТЕБЯ ПИСЬМА, НО ОКАЗАЛОСЬ...
...ЕНИЦ ЕСТЬ РУМЫНСКИЕ ДЕВОЧКИ 7 И 8 ЛЕТ. И ВОТ Я ВЗЯЛА НА СЕБЯ...
...ИТЬ ИХ РУССКОЙ АЗБУКЕ. УСПЕХИ КОЛОССАЛЬНЫЕ (КОНЕ...
...РЕМЕННО ОНИ МЕНЯ "УЧАТ" РУМЫНСКОМУ. ПРИ ОБХОДЕ...
...АК ХОРОШО ЧИТАЛИ, ЧТО МНЕ КАК-ТО ХОРОШО И ПРИЯТНО...
...КОМ МОЕМ ПОЯВЛЕНИИ ОНИ МЕНЯ СПРАШИВАЮТ, А БУДУ ЛИ Я ИХ УЧИТЬ ЕЩЕ?!! В...
...БРЯ БЫЛ У НАС ВЕЧЕР НА РАБОТЕ, НА КОТОРОМ Я ПЕЛА "ЖУРАВЛИ" И ПРОЧЕЕ. ВСПО...
...ЛА НАШУ ЖИЗНЬ В ПРАГЕ И КАК-ТО СТАЛО ГРУСТНО-ГРУСТНО. ВЕДЬ СКОЛЬКО...
...РЕЧАЕМСЯ. ВСЕ НАМ ПРИХОДИТСЯ КУДА-ТО СПЕШИТЬ И ВСЕ У НАС НЕ ХВАТАЕТ...
...СНИ: ВСПОМНИЛА ПРЕДПОСЛЕДНИЙ ДЕНЬ, ПРОВЕДЕННЫЙ В ПРАГЕ, А ОСОБЕННО...
...НЕ НЕ ДАЮТ ПОКОЯ, КАК-ТО ТЯЖЕЛО И ГРУСТНО СТАЛО ИХ ПЕТЬ. ДОМА У НАС...
...ТАРОМУ. ЛИЗА МЕНЯ В ЭТОЙ ЧЕТВЕРТИ ОЧЕНЬ ОГОРЧИЛА. ПЕРВЫЙ РАЗ ЗА ВСЕ...
...ЧТОБЫ ЛИЗА ПРИНЕСЛА 4-Е ТРОЙКИ: ПО ГЕОМЕТРИИ, АЛГЕБРЕ, АНГЛИЙСКОМУ И...
...УРЕ, ОСТАЛЬНЫЕ ЧЕТВЕРКИ. ТЫ НЕ ПРЕДСТАВЛЯЕШЬ, КАК Я РАССТРОИЛАСЬ, ВЕДЬ НЕ...
...РИ ИНСТИТУТ. ДИМА ПРИНЕС ЕЩЕ ХУЖЕ ОТМЕТКИ, ВКЛЮЧАЯ ДИСЦИПЛИНУ И ПРИ...
...Е. 7-ОГО Я БЫЛА У РИМЫ И ИГОРЯ. ВЕЧЕР ПРОШЕЛ ОЧЕНЬ ХОРОШО. БЫЛО 14 ЧЕЛОВ...
...ТРОЙКИ: ВЫПИЛИ ЗА ТЕБЯ. ВСЕ ТЕБЯ ВСПОМИНАЮТ ДОБРЫМИ СЛОВАМИ. НО...
...СТОЯЛ И ПРОСЬБЕ МАРИНЫ И ВСЕХ ПРИСУТСТВУЮЩИХ Я СПЕЛА ОПЯТЬ-ТАКИ "ЖУРА...

...СЕБЕ, ПРОИЗВЕЛА ВПЕЧАТЛЕНИЕ НА ВСЕХ, НИКТО НЕ ДУМАЛ, ЧТО...
...НЕМНОГО УМЕЮ...ВСЕ МЫ ОЧЕНЬ ОГОРЧИЛИСЬ, ЧТО НЕ БЫЛО ТЕБЯ, А ОСОБЕННО...
...ВЕДЬ СКОЛЬКО...НЕ ИЗМЕНЯЕТ МНЕ ПАМЯТЬ, ТО УЖЕ 7 ОКТЯБРЬСКИХ И 6 НОВЫХ...
...НАШИХ ПРАЗДНИКОВ — ЭТО НЕ ВКЛЮЧАЯ ПРОЧИХ ФАМИЛЬНЫХ ТОРЖЕСТВ. Я...
...ОНА!! КАК НЕСПРАВЕДЛИВА ЖИЗНЬ. Я ВСЕ ПОНИМАЮ, ЧТО ТЫ РАБОТАЕШЬ, И ЧТО ЭТО...
...ТВОЙ ДОЛГ И ЧТО ТЫ ЛЮБИШЬ СВОЮ РАБОТУ И ОЧЕНЬ ДОБРОСОВЕСТНО ОТНОСИШЬСЯ КО...
...ВСЕМУ ЭТОМУ, НО ТЕМ НЕ МЕНЕЕ Я КАК-ТО ЧИСТО ПО-ОБЫВАТЕЛЬСКИ РАССУЖДАЮ (ПО...
...ЖЕНСКИ). СТРАДАЮ, СТРАШУСЬ СВОЕГО ОДИНОЧЕСТВА. И ВОТ — ЭТО ВСЕ ОСОБЕННО ПРО...
...ОДИТСЯ ВО МНЕ, КОГДА НАСТУПАЮТ КАКИЕ-НИБУДЬ ПРАЗДНЕСТВА. Я ВСЕГДА РАДУЮСЬ...
...КОГДА КОНЧАЕТСЯ ПРАЗДНИК И НАСТУПАЕТ ОБЫЧНЫЙ РАБОЧИЙ ДЕНЬ. Я КАК-ТО СЕБЯ...
...ЧУВСТВУЮ ИНАЧЕ, КАК БУДТО БЫСТРЕЙ КОНЧАЕТСЯ И НАЧИНАЕТСЯ ДЕНЬ. ДОЕХАЛА Я ХО...
...ШО. ВСЕ БЫЛО ТАК, КАК ТЫ МНЕ ГОВОРИЛ, ТАК ЧТО Я НАПРАСНО ВОЛНОВАЛАСЬ. ВЕРА...
...МА УПАЛА ЗА НЕДЕЛЮ ДО ПРАЗДНИКА И СЛОМАЛА НОГУ В ЛОДЫЖКЕ. СЕЙЧАС ОНА...
...ПСЕ. БАБУШКА ИЗ ПАДАЕТ С НОГ, К ТОМУ ЖЕ ЮРА ЗАБОЛЕЛ ВОСПАЛЕНИЕМ ЛЕГКИХ. ЭТО...
...ЧНО. ЭТО ВСЕ ЖДЕТ НАШЕГО СЫНА (ВСЯКИЕ БЕСКОНЕЧНЫЕ БОЛЕЗНИ). НАДО, ДОРОГОЙ...
...ОЙ. ПОДУМАТЬ ХОРОШО О ДЕТСКОМ САДЕ?! ТРОФИМУ БОЛЕТЬ СОВЕРШЕННО НЕЖЕЛАТЕЛЬ...
...О. ДО СВИДАНИЯ, ДОРОГОЙ МОЙ И ХОРОШИЙ, САМЫЙ ЛЮБИМЫЙ И БЛИЗКИЙ МНЕ ЧЕЛОВЕК...
...ЛЮБЛЮ ТЕБЯ. ПИШИ МНЕ, КАК СЕБЯ ЧУВСТВУЕШЬ, ПИШИ, ЧТО ЛЮБИШЬ МЕНЯ, МОЖЕТ МНЕ...
...УДЕТ ЛУЧШЕ. Д... ПРОЗА!!! ЕСЛИ ВОЗМОЖНО, ТО Я ТЕБЯ ПРОШУ ДАВАТЬ МНЕ 2500...
...УАЛЕЙ В МЕСЯЦ.

/XI-60.../ ЗДРАВСТВУЙ, ДОРОГОЙ ПАПОЧКА! ПОЗДРАВЛЯЮ ТЕБЯ С 43 ГОДОВЩИНОЙ ОК...
...КАК ТЫ СЕБЯ ЧУВСТВУЕШЬ? МЫ ВСЕ ЗДОРОВЫ. ЗАВТРА МЫ ЕДЕМ К ТЕТЕ...

21

CHAPTER
4

STEGANOGRAPHY IN DIGITAL MEDIA

The digital era has brought new life to steganography. Using steganography, messages can be embedded into image, video, and audio files. These are called stego-media files.

Steganography is often used to embed information in image files. One way to do this is by changing the brightness of a pixel. Pixels are tiny squares of color. Image files can be made up of thousands of pixels.

The most common pixel format measures brightness from 0 to 255. The number 0 indicates no brightness, or black. The number 255 indicates full brightness, or white.

Two images may look identical. But a pixel in one image might have a brightness of 200. The same pixel's brightness in the other image might have been changed to 201. The human eye cannot see this difference. But the change could communicate something in a secret messaging system.

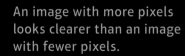

An image with more pixels looks clearer than an image with fewer pixels.

In this close-up image, each square of color is a pixel.

People once used telegraphs and Morse code to transmit messages over long distances.

In 2016, a Polish researcher embedded information into dance music by changing its tempo. Krzysztof Szczypiorski sped up or slowed down each beat of the song "Rhythm is a Dancer" by less than 1 percent. Changes this small cannot be detected by the human ear.

Szczypiorski's study found that even musicians could not detect a 2 percent tempo change.

By changing each beat's tempo, Szczypiorski created a series of longer and shorter beats. These translated into Morse Code! Morse Code assigns a set of dots, or short beats, and dashes, or long beats, to each letter in the English alphabet. Using long and short beats, Szczypiorski spelled out the message, "Steganography is a dancer," over the course of the song.

This image was one of several used by Russian spies to send secret information overseas.

Anna Chapman was one of the accused Russian spies from the 2010 spy ring.

The invention of computers and the internet has brought many opportunities to society. But these innovations have also introduced cybercrime. Stego-media files are sometimes used to hide criminal information.

In 2010, the FBI uncovered a Russian spy ring that had been sending illegal information using steganography. Eleven spies posing as US citizens were arrested.

The group of spies had been sending information to a foreign intelligence department in Moscow, Russia. This information included secrets about US nuclear weapons research. The intelligence department had created its own steganography software that allowed the spies to embed information into digital images.

In the future, cybersecurity experts predict steganography could be used to hide harmful computer programs.

CONCLUSION

Steganography has been used to conceal information since ancient times. From microdots to stego-media files, steganography has adapted to new technology.

Today, there are hundreds of free steganography software programs available to try. As the world becomes more connected, opportunities grow for steganographers to try their skills.

Crack It! Make Your Own Cardan Grille ⟶•

Materials
three sheets of letter paper
scissors
pen or pencil

1. Write a short message on a sheet of paper. Space each word out randomly on the page.

2. Use a ruler to measure the length and location of each word in the message.

3. Using these measurements, cut a hole for each word in a second sheet of paper. This paper is your grille.

4. Place your grille over a third sheet of paper. Write your message in the holes and remove the grille.

5. On the third sheet of paper, fill in the spaces around the words with sentences. When finished, your letter will look normal. But placing the grille over the letter will reveal your original message!

Dear Laura,

I have been playing lots of tennis, which I know is your favorite sport. Where do you usually play?

My mom says you are great! I wanted to play yesterday but Kai hid my racket. It was the first time I didn't like him, but then we made cookies and made up.

from Ainslee

GLOSSARY

chemical reaction: a chemical change that happens when two things combine to form a new substance

cipher: a message in which individual letters are changed to conceal the message's meaning

code: a message in which words or phrases are changed to conceal the message's meaning

compound: something created when two or more parts are joined together

cybercrime: criminal activity in which a computer is used to illegally access, send, or change data

innovation: a new device or idea

invoice: a document that shows a list of purchased goods and the prices paid for them

rebel: to oppose or fight against an authority

recipient: someone who receives something

LEARN MORE

BBC Bitesize: How Do Digital Images Work?
https://www.bbc.co.uk/bitesize/topics/zf2f9j6/articles/z2tgr82

Boyer, Crispin. *Top Secret.* Washington: National Geographic Kids, 2020.

Caswell, Deanna. *Making Secret Codes and Messages.* Mankato, MN: Black Rabbit Books, 2019.

Hunt, Elizabeth Singer. *Secret Agent Training Manual: How to Make and Break Top Secret Messages.* New York: Weinstein Books, 2017.

Thomas, Rachael L. *Classic Codes and Ciphers.* Minneapolis: Lerner Publications, 2022.

Wonderopolis: How Does Invisible Ink Work?
https://wonderopolis.org/wonder/how-does-invisible-ink-work-2

INDEX